Buffaloes

Marianne Johnston

The Rosen Publishing Group's
PowerKids Press™
New York

Published in 1997 by The Rosen Publishing Group, Inc.
29 East 21st Street, New York, NY 10010

First Edition

Book Design: Kim Sonsky

Photo Credits: front cover © Kevin Sink/MIDWESTOCK; pp. 4–5, 8, 14 © Rick Adair/MIDWESTOCK; p. 6 © David Morris/MIDWESTOCK; pp. 7, 13, and back cover © Eric Berndt/MIDWESTOCK; p. 11 © Jim Hays/MIDWESTOCK; p. 17 © Kevin Anderson/MIDWESTOCK; p. 18 © Corbis–Bettmann; p. 21 © 1996 PhotoDisc, Inc.

Johnston, Marianne.
    Buffaloes / Marianne Johnston.
        p.   cm. — (The giant animals series)
    Includes index.
    Summary: Describes what buffaloes look like, what they eat, where they live and how they have been treated by Native Americans and other people.
    ISBN 0-8239-5147-2 (lib. bdg.)
    1. American bison—Juvenile literature. [1. Bison.] I. Title. II. Series: Johnston, Marianne. Giant animals series.
QL737.U53J67 1996
599.64'3'0973—DC21   96-47917
                                                                                  CIP
                                                                                   AC

Manufactured in the United States of America

CONTENTS

THE BUFFALO

The buffalo is one of the strongest and most powerful animals in North America. Buffaloes are also called **bison** (BY-sun). Millions of buffaloes once lived all over the United States, Canada, and Mexico. Now there

▲ Buffaloes live mostly in the western part of the United States.

are far fewer buffaloes. Today, they live mostly in national parks and protected areas in Oklahoma, North Dakota, South Dakota, Wyoming, and Canada. These huge, fur-covered animals can run as fast as 35 miles an hour.

TWO KINDS OF BUFFALOES

There are two kinds of buffaloes: the European buffalo and the American buffalo. The European buffalo is a little bit smaller than the American buffalo. This kind of buffalo lives in the forests of Europe. The American buffalo lives in the United States and Canada. Most of the buffaloes in the United States live on open land called **plains** (PLAYNZ). Buffaloes in Canada live in forests. They live to be about 25 years old. This book will talk mostly about the American buffalo.

The American buffalo lives on the plains and in the forests of North America. ▶
▼

6

WHAT DO THEY LOOK LIKE?

A buffalo is a very large animal that looks sort of like a bull. It has a large hump on its back that is close to its shoulder. The head of a buffalo is very large. On males it looks even bigger than it really is because of a long beard that hangs from the face.

A grown-up male buffalo can be six feet tall and ten to fourteen feet long. The biggest buffaloes weigh almost 3,000 pounds!

◀ A buffalo's horns can grow up to six feet long.

BUFFALO FUR

A buffalo's fur is mostly dark brown with some patches of black. In the front of the buffalo's body, the fur can grow almost two feet long. The fur on the back end of the body is shorter. A buffalo's fur is also very thick and warm. Buffaloes need thick winter coats to keep them warm in places like Wyoming, where it can get as cold as 40°F below zero! But when the weather gets warm, the buffalo **sheds** (SHEDZ) a lot of its coat.

The buffalo sheds its thick winter coat in the spring. ▶

10

WHAT DOES A BUFFALO EAT?

The buffalo is a **grazer** (GRAY-zer). This means it eats plants that grow on the ground. In the summer it also eats herbs and grass.

During the winter, piles of snow cover the grass on the ground. To get to its food, the buffalo swings its huge head back and forth to brush away the snow.

Buffaloes usually eat in the morning or in the evening.

The buffalo uses his large head and beard to uncover food hidden in the snow. ▶

HOW DOES A BUFFALO EAT?

When you eat something, you chew it in your mouth and then swallow it. After that it goes down to your stomach.

The buffalo eats this way, too. But after the buffalo has swallowed its food, it comes back up from its stomach and into its mouth. The buffalo chews it again and then swallows it again. This is called chewing a **cud** (KUD). It's almost like eating twice!

When the buffalo chews its cud, the food is easier to eat.

15

YOUNG BUFFALOES

Most baby buffaloes are born in May, when the weather is warm. When the baby is born, its eyes are open. A baby buffalo weighs between 30 and 70 pounds. People weigh only about seven pounds when they are born.

Baby buffaloes, called **calves** (KAVZ), can stand and drink milk from their mothers an hour after being born. A calf is usually a red or yellow color. Mothers are very **protective** (pro-TEK-tiv) of their calves. They keep them safe from other animals.

Buffalo calves stay close to their mothers when they are young. ▶

16

THE BUFFALOES AND THE NATIVE AMERICANS

Long ago, the buffaloes played an important part in the lives of the Plains Indians, one of the many groups of Native Americans in the West. Buffaloes were an important part of their religion, food, shelter, and clothing. Native American tribes such as the Sioux, Crow, Apache, and Cheyenne had great **respect** (ree-SPEKT) for buffaloes. Native Americans never killed a buffalo unless they needed to. They used every part of the animal. They ate its meat and made needles, knives, arrowheads, and even dice from its bones. It took fifteen buffalo **hides** (HYDZ) to make one teepee, or house.

Native Americans used buffalo hides to make their houses.

19

WHAT HAPPENED TO THE BUFFALOES?

In 1871 there were 60 million buffaloes. Twenty years later, fewer than 1,000 were left. What happened to the buffaloes?

American **settlers** (SET-lerz) killed millions of buffaloes. Some were killed to feed the workers who were building railroads in the West. Many were killed as a way of hurting the Native Americans who needed the buffaloes to survive. These settlers almost caused the **extinction** (ex-TEENKT-shun) of buffaloes.

Long ago, American settlers almost destroyed all of the buffaloes. ▶

THE BUFFALO RETURNS

People decided that it was time to help the buffaloes. Before the last few could be killed, the American **government** (GUV-ern-ment) passed laws to protect the few that were left. In 1890, land in Yellowstone National Park in Wyoming was set aside just for buffaloes. Four years later, hunting buffaloes in Yellowstone was against the law. In 1905 the American Bison Society was started to help protect the **endangered** (en-DAYN-jehrd) buffalo. Today about 140,000 buffaloes live in the United States and Canada.

GLOSSARY

bison (BY-sun) Buffalo.

calf (KAF) A young buffalo.

cud (KUD) The food that is brought back up from the stomach to be chewed again.

endangered (en-DAYN-jehrd) When something has very few of its kind left.

extinction (ex-TEENKT-shun) Bringing something to the point where there are none left.

government (GUV-ern-ment) The people who rule a state or country.

grazer (GRAY-zer) An animal that eats grass and plants from the ground.

hide (HYD) The skin of an animal.

plains (PLAYNZ) Long, flat areas of land.

protective (pro-TEK-tiv) Keeping something from harm.

respect (ree-SPEKT) To admire someone.

settler (SET-ler) A person who comes to live in a new area.

shed (SHED) To get rid of.

INDEX